I0143190

In My Feelings Poetry

Honey Luscious

Copyright © 2015 Honey Luscious
Liberation's publishing ~ West Point, MS
All rights reserved.
ISBN-13: 978-0692371374
ISBN-10: 0692371370

I love hard. But when I'm done, I'm done!
~ Honey Luscious~

Table of contents

A woman never stops loving you.
She just chooses to love herself more.
~Honey Luscious~

What If...

What if…
We hadn't met, would there be any regret

What if…
I had to choose, and there was no win or lose

What if…
I didn't love you so, and decided to let you go

What if…
You made me cry, and I decided to no longer give it a try

What if…
The what if died, then you'd know our love I'd never defy

Somethings aren't meant to be,
Except you and me that's why there are no What if's

Mr. Right...

As I search the depths of my soul

Longing for Mr. Right to come make me whole

There's someone waiting beyond the sunrise and sunset

Who needs to be loved by the best

Does good love really make you cry

Or does it make you feel like you're loving the wrong guy

My need for love can't get any stronger

So I guess I'll wait a little longer

Untrue...

As I sit here and contemplate...

Where did I go wrong?

Where did I make my mistake?

Where did I go wrong?

Is it too late?

How do I right my wrong?

Do I try to hold on?

I can't think

My mind is in the zone

Never wanted to relive the past

I know it's not going to last

This love for you is untrue

I can't be with you

This is goodbye and I understand why

I'm here and you're there

This love we don't share

I'm not anyone's spare

Just remember another (you can't) dare compare

Love is...

Love is like a baby

You can't think perhaps or maybe

It can be as gentle as a lamb'

Or can explode with a bam

It can be a winning game

Or make your life a living shame

Love is like a hidden treasure

That no one can measure

Each moment you I will miss

That's why I leave it sealed in a erotic kiss

Love is what you make it

That's why I take no shit

This wonderful day...

As I stand here on this wonderful day

Is there any other way for me to say

You are filling a void, making me your one and only

This day is what I dreamed of

Realizing you were sent from heaven above

This is not a dream

But an everlasting love no one can come between

The simplest prayer can come true

Just like saying I do

Just like being near you

This is a wonderful day

Charges...

As a love wanted criminal who committed a crime

How would you spend the time

Will the judge through your charges out quick

Not labeling you a convict

Because there was not enough evidence

Your love for me is evident

You're sure to get not guilty

Or resting on appeal

For loving a touch or a feel

No man should experience jail

For loving a girl that loves him for real

Our best...

Am I right?

Are you right?

Is my heart, where you belong?

Why do we try?

Must we deny?

How will we know?

When to let got

What will we show?

How will we confide?

Where will we reside,

Love is only what we make of it

That's why I won't quit.

Till love is what we really got.

And we give it our best shot

I'll handle the rest...

See I been watching you for a while

And I'm digging your style

Think I'll make a step so I can see

If you could be the one for me

Try and make this a possibility

I see you watching me too

Which is why I stepped to you

Don't deny what you feel

Just open up so you can feel

This seductive hot intimacy

That comes from inside of me

All you got to do is say yes

Lay back and I'll handle the rest

Finally...

I'm so proud to be standing here today

Been waiting to hear you say

We can finally have it our way

You for me and me for you

Our dream is about to come true

I never gave up looking for my mate

I didn't find you too late

If one should try to question

Let this be a good lesson

That it takes a very long wait

To get from dam good to dam great

My prince has finally arrived

I no longer have to strive

You are the one that makes my heart cry

Tears of joy that I can't deny

You were truly sent from above

And this is a strong love

One that was built on trust, honor and respect

Our relationship I'd never neglect

Love etiquette #1029...

My heart longs for a passionate love

That can make my heart soar like a morning dove

Every time I see your face

I imagine us in a special place

The intimate times we share

No one can dare compare

Our love is like a rare but old wine

That's tasteful yet hard to define

None other can come close

This is more potent that any doctors written dose

No longer resist...

There's nothing grander

Than a man who will stand

For what his heart desires

I love to hear your sexy voice

That reminds me of the day I made the right choice

Try it if you dare

You can't come close so don't try to compare

To this love I've found

It's like being on a merry go round

My love does exist

I wore you down till you could no longer resist

Queen Bee...

I can see you when I close my eyes

These feelings I can't deny

Each day I do my best

Cause this diva settles for nothing less

I will let you touch everything I am

No this ain't no wham bam thank you mam

I'm Miss Queen B you see

There's no one else better than me

Rest...

No longer do you have to fight

The temptation of another lonely night

For out of the darkness came

The man who wanted to proclaim

The love your heart was destined to capture and maintain

There are no words to verify

The everlasting sparkle he brings to your eye

No more of me...

I'm not the first or last

You're just a blast from my past

There's no more hurting over you

I can find someone better who will do

All the things I need

No baby it's not about greed

I just refuse to stop

My love was good to the last drop

Once you hit the spot

You wanted another shot

Just let go

You and I are no more

So good bye and hit the door

You ain't never...

You ain't never had it done by me before.

You ain't never had it done by the best. I know.

Fooling with me I will make you believe

You've died and gone to heaven, want me to conceive

Now I am down

Shit, have you helping me choose that white wedding gown

I'm the hottest thing next to the sun

No you're not jumping the gun

This time you'll know that you've got the right one

I'll have you running red lights, sleep walking at night

After me no other will there be

You are my soul mate we were destined to be

Bad guy...

Cool, suave, romantic and smooth talking

That's what I want, without stalking

A kiss that will make me melt

Love like this I've never felt

A touch as chilling as a block of ice

This guy should be like a pair of loaded dice

Always out to win

He's like a shot of gin

Wants to go again and again

This guy is like no other

But not a guy to meet your mother

His intentions will always be misunderstood

But only if they could know and see his good

I know he's a winner

Cause he tore up that spot in the center

Unleashed...

You've figured it out I guess

Fucking with me is just like playing chess

I won't stop til I am crowned the best

How can you want to take it a step farther?

Knowing I'm the one you take home to meet mother

I try to always remain

An angel in disguise til you stop going insane

From the effects of the love I've laid

I'm a new car why think about trade

Somehow you bring out the beast

Yes its true a panther you've unleashed

That heat...

Can you make this thing sang a song

I doubt it. I heard it won't last long

Three to five

Is how long it's alive

That is minutes not hours

Man you need some real power

This ain't no play thing

I need a man to ring

My bell (that is), beat the drum

I want to end it in a deep hum

A sweet but short moan and groan

I want to feel the fire

That you get in a heated desire

This could happen without a doubt

Every now and then everyone needs to shout

Have mercy, oh god, help me lord

Church ain't the only place

That you can sing Amazing Grace

My guy...

As I sit here on this day in 2008

Cause I finally found my ideal mate

Tall, dark, handsome and out of sight

This time I got Mr. Right

I no longer have to search

He's within arm's length to touch

No longer shall I try

To sit, wait, and wonder why

You're truly mine, my guy

Lover's ease...

If you choose me

I can set your body free

I just want to feel the bed shake

I need to hear you say "for goodness sake"

She don't treat you right

You always uptight

I hear it in your voice

That you made the wrong choice

It tears me up inside to see the tears in your eyes

Baby why continue to deny

You living a lie

That she don't know how

Today I make the vow

The man of my dreams

Should be made to scream

Left with a linger of the night

I stepped in his sight

The day I let him taste

What he'll be letting go to waste

The times we are apart

There's a pain in his heart

Cause (me) I'm his pill

For what makes him ill

I'm the cure

To the disease

Called LOVERS EASE

Madina Madness...

You had a girl, but she just wasn't me

Someone who made you feel as if you had drifted in the sea

She just couldn't grip that tip, squeeze and please

You had a girl, but she couldn't take that Madina you called a snake

You had a girl but she just didn't have what it takes

Shake and shiver as if you had a cold

Make that pussy grab and hold

Make you cry and call on God and ask him why

Now if want this all the time

You have to let her go to have mine

Or you get no more of this spectacular ride

No other good as me...

Say you want put that madina on me

Well just wait and see

That this can't be

You found your match

You got the right catch

No twist, no grind, no groan

I'm a woman standing on her own

That is working it, stroking it, and giving it back

I don't need no assistance I'm taking up the slack

Don't you know and can't you see

That there's not another good as me

A life-long search...

The time I spent on this lifelong search

In the streets, club and church

For my soul mate

No one can anticipate

The anguish of lonely nights

Praying for a bright shining light

No one can understand the tears you cry

Waiting for that ideal guy

Not just anyone will do

There has to be some chemistry to attract him to you

Now that the search is over

You've found your own chocolate four leaf clover

Charming...

If I waited on the end of the rainbow

Then my true love I would never know

I need for him to be as good as gold

My prince charming

Will always keep it real and alarming

His smile will be as bright as the sun

That will be your protection and gun

The touch of his hand

Will be like a walk in the sand

So soothing and free

At least we finally have a chance for awesome treat

Like the still of the night

This is truly and most definitely right

Lover's creed...

I feel as if you were drawn to me

That we were destining to be

Time well spent

Was our intent

Time well kept

As we slipped and crept

Surely we are in the right place

Cause we named it Lovers Space

No ones to blame

So we feel no shame

I can't let go, nor set you free

Cause our love is all I see

This is our lover's creed

Potion motion...

I wanna wrap my legs around your waist

Alone in a dark place

And give you a taste

We gotta do this in slow motion

As if we'd been given a love potion

There's one thing to realize

Someone tries to analyze

Of how we could be

Just tell them to wait and see

We'll be in love for eternity

No regrets...

There are no words to explain

The love for you I proclaim

I often think of how else this could be

But somehow you made me see

That we are truly destine to be

A kiss as soft as a kind word

Your word as sweet as a humming bird

Today I stand here on this day

In happiness of my wedding waiting to say

Here is where I want to remain and stay

I do is all that's needed to be said

Because we are and always will be in read

No other way will I have it

This is as good as it gets

I will choose forever without any regrets

The game...

How much longer should I endure?

The enticement of your allure

The pain from this lover's game

I'm not the blame, I feel no shame

Even though you don't refrain

From wanting to put a hurting on this thang

I can understand why

I never should have given you a try

Sometimes it may spiral out of control

let love take charge of your soul

I'm not going to lie

This love is sure to make you cry

I'll say I'm sorry and you'll accept

Then you will know why Jesus wept

The concept for this is love is like a game of spade

You'll figure it out, I just got played

Boy toy...

You're so enticing to me

I had to make my move if it was to be

You and I sitting in the sunset hand in hand

Dam it's too good, are you really my man

Don't pinch me because I might wake

And say what's wrong for goodness sake

I've had enough sadness

Being alone there's nothing seriously wrong

But having someone has truly made me strong

There's nothing that I can't do

To have it to be and you

Why is there so much joy?

I have my manly boy toy

Bliss...

You and I were destine to be

In a special place created by you and me

No longer do I have to hide

The true feelings I hold inside

I want the world to know

That you gave my face this glow

I want the world to see

That you are the Mr. Right for me

I want the world to witness

This joyful bliss, just as I did on our first date and kiss

When we are together the world stops in time

It's as if we keep it on rewind

No we ain't in the club

It's sort of like being in a steamy hot tub

Insist...

Is love such a big deal

That you question if it's really real

Does it leave you on a wing

Make you feel like a hot fling

When the guy starts to insist

That you tie the knot rather than resist

You start to question his actions

Of why this reaction

Don't drink and look

Cause this will happen every time

He'll be hooked

This won't be the last time

You'll be getting them at the drop of a dime

Better with time...

Never thought the time would come

I'd find someone that could make my heart hum

Hum a tune so sweet

 And soft as a baby's pattering feet

Never thought I could feel as if I could steal

Something as awesome as your love

Which is as amazing as a morning dove

Never thought I would find

Someone to make me feel as good as rare wine

That only gets better and ages with time

Heartache...

There are no words to explain

My heartache and pain

The love I longed for

Is now no more

It was short, but sweet

Dam I'm glad it ended in a heartbeat

The anguish I had to endure

Was too much for any I'm sure

You were seeking a fool,

but I was too advanced and schooled

Try to run your game

On someone who's good and lame

I had the qualification to maintain

But the heartache was too much pain

Believe me...

Heartbroken and sad

I'm also glad

That this is no more

The same one I tried to adore

I gave the door

There was no love loss

For I needed you to know I'm the boss

Tried to convince myself

That after you there would be no one else

It's over and I need no one to convince me

That this is over can't you see

Fill the gap...

As I sit and reminisce

On the love I long for and miss

You came and filled a gap

That could have lingered on, no, well perhaps

I have found such joy in sharing something as delicate as Rose

When you made me cry, as you broke down and propose

There is no way for me to explain

Forever is what we will remain

Lover's bliss...

How could this be?

Was love meant for you and me?

Time will tell

Into the sunset we will sail

There will be no turning back

that's a promise not a fact

Each day will be a fight

But to love we must hold on tight

For the time we're apart

We'll seal it with a kiss

For you I'll truly miss

This is my lovers' bliss

Paused...

You and I were destine to be

In a special place created by you and me

No longer do I have to hide

The true feelings I hold inside

I want the world to know

That you gave my face this glow

I want the world to see

That you are the Mr. Right for me

I want the world to witness

This joyful bliss, just as I did on our first kiss

When we are together the world stops in time

No need to press play no need to rewind

If my heart could speak...

If my heart could speak

It would tell of the special one I seek

If my heart could express

It would be of your beauty and soft caress

If my heart could touch

It would feel so much

If my heart could confess

I'm better than all the rest

If my heart could taste

It would be like of a silky paste

The brightness of a rainbow

So exquisite only you would know

Daydream...

With you is where I'm destined to be

Overlooking some city

Gazing into one another eyes

Forgetting about sad goodbyes

We have nothing else to fear

We're shifted into high gear

Never to think of the past

For true love we have at last

What I need...

How do I begin to miss?

The hot passionate linger of your kiss

I try so hard to search and find

My lifelong mate to call mine

Is he really waiting for me?

Or is loneliness my destiny

The key lies in me

Keep searching until I see

Sexy, romantic, outgoing, irresistible

No need to explain

I cannot make it anymore plain

Straight to the point

I don't want a thug straight out the joint

I need a man to hit the spot

And always keep it hot

Why...

There are times I ask the question why

why I can't do anything to satisfy

The man I finally found to share

The good, romantic, and sexy somewhere

A love that is so hard to let go

Why won't you let me show...

You all I have to give

With you is where my heart longs to live

Without you my life will be incomplete

That day my heart will refuse to beat

I've come too far to give up now

I pray to God we can make it somehow

I need to know you will continue to fight

Cause this love we have is right

The high and low of it...

Love sometimes is like a shower

That can last long getting colder by the hour

Love is only what you make of it

It has good and wonderful benefits

Love can be like a penny you save

Over time it becomes a dollar

Love can feel like you're trapped in a cave

All alone making you want to holler

Love can be the grandest thing

Better than some hot quick fling

Loving you has made me realize

That I no longer have to fantasize

Over what it feels like to love

We're living it day by day

Highs and lows, blow by blows in love

When my prince comes...

Why must it be this way?

Why must I wait another day

I need my prince to rescue me

He'll know we are destined to be

We'll travel together on this bumpy ride

We'll make it, God will be our guide

I refuse to give in

My heart will not always be broken

Waiting...

Why do I sit here and contemplate

 Have I waited too dam late

I try not to think why

I keep telling myself continue to try

This is a great place to begin

To start the healing from within

Because true love is like a ocean ride

You can swim or get taken away by the tide

I just know I want let go

My prince will soon be at the door

Awesome...

The day I found you my search was over

It was like searching a field for a four leaf clovers

I wouldn't settle for anything less

For me you are the very best

It had to be excellent, awesome and grand

Like room of exquisite jewels and my wonderful man

To us another cannot compare

It hot and warm and so much to share

Adventure...

Where have you been all my life

 I'm glad you're making me your wife

This is my chance of a lifetime

From now own you'll be all mine

I stand here today

I say yes we're on our way

The joy I feel

Couldn't be any more real

As we set out on this adventure

We will experience something so spectacular

That no one can touch or capture

You for me and me for you

We are a dream come true

Now you got someone...

I can see it in your eyes

But I understand why

You look so long

To understand (for you) she was wrong

I don't know why

Your heart has to cry

You never had someone:

To do you properly

That's me

You never had someone:

To give you what you been waiting for

There's a grand treasure in store

You never had someone:

To say it's yours

Do what you please

I know you're hurting

But baby don't you worry

I'll always hurry

To give you what you been waiting for

You ain't had never had someone to lay you down

Starting on the bed and finishing up on the ground

You ain't ever had someone?

That's all about your needs

That's woman is me ... Now You Got Someone

Searching...

It's going to hurt to say goodbye

I can't understand why

I can't find the love

That is as gentle as a morning dove

the love my heart and soul desires

the love that always has the fire

Many nights have I cried

Many nights Jesus wiped my eyes

The heartache I endured was sure

I didn't lose sight I did endure

Though I walked alone in the night

At the end of the tunnel there was light

I have peace of mind

I'm victorious the soldier in me shines

I have come so far and I refuse to give in

There is no victory in sin

In the end I always win

Your voice...

As the night grows near

My heart can hear

The deep soft whisper of your voice

Calling out saying I am the right choice

How can I find you, without getting lost?

Just be willing to keep going on matter what the cost

I have the motive and initiative to keep going

Without even knowing

Without any care

Of what will happen

I'm always up for a dare

This makes the chase more intense

Sort of like a movies sequel, or should I say suspense

Stop denying...

Why must I continue to try?

To be with this guy

He doesn't have a clue?

That here stands a love so true

Why must I render

When he doesn't want a love so tender

Why must I confess?

When he's in distress

From continually trying to defy

The love for me that shows in his eyes

The time we spend trying to hold it in

Makes the fire and passion hotter when we let go and give in

To become lovers not strangers

Let her go and we'll be in no danger

Dreaming...

Is my heart where you're destine to be

That's what my friends ask me

I just sit, think, and stare

And imagine my life without you there

No greater choice could I have made

Props to the future for nothing I will trade

To have it any other way

Until we walk the aisle on our wedding day

I know it will happen soon

On one warm summer afternoon

The sun will be going down

We'll gave all our loved ones around

This will be the best in town

You in your tux and me in my spunky cream grown

Breath...

My life was like a ship lost at sea

Until you came and rescued me

Before there were no trips

Now that you are the captain on this ship

No longer am I afraid

This is a journey I wouldn't trade

The tide can stand up high

For we are like the birds soaring in the sky

This I can say

We can set sail

And I can now exhale

Spice...

Why can't you just agree?

There's more too than just sexing me

My smile, beauty and charm

But just don't trigger off the alarm

There's one thing I must confess

I'm better than good… dam I'm the best

A kiss, a touch

Is that too much

Hell no

It's just too let you know

I like to be kissed and licked from head to toe

You gave all you got

You hit the right spot

Til you get it right...

How man licks does it take?

To make my body shiver and shake

How many bites

Til you get it right

How many strokes

To get the steady poke

Do I need to wish you luck?

Or must I instruct

I won't groan

Til I hear you moan

I won't say quit

Til you hit the right lick

Let me tell it...

You and I are destine to be

A special created by you and me

No longer do I have to hide

The true feelings I hold inside

I want to world to know

That you gave my gave this glow

I want the world to see

That you are the Mr. Right for me

I want the world to witness

This joyfully bliss like our first kiss

When we are together the world stops in time

It's as if we keep it on rewind

Arrest me...

Better that the best

I won't settle for anything les

You can be my umbrella when it rains

I can be your psychiatrist when you're going insane

You can be the officer to charge me with a crime

I am guilty I will do the time

You can be my hero

Cause there's no place here for a zero

Drink...

I will be your drink of water

When you thirst

I will be the sun that shines

When your days are dark

I will be your strength

When you are weak

I will be your map

When you have no direction

These things I vow here today

Never will either of us stray

Careful steps...

Here I sit feeling my life in such a shamble

Or should I say like a deck of cards, a gamble

I pray to God for goodness sake

Not to fall apart with the steps I take

Everyone's got their own thoughts about me

I can prove them wrong in end you'll see

I know I'm an original with the actions I show,

But only me and God really know

Settled....

As there anyone who can profess

The love we share is no contest

Is there anyone who can compare?

A love more grand or rare

Is there anyone who can see?

The inner and outer beauty you bring out of me

Is there anyone who can love this way?

I thank God for together we will stay

There is no other that I'd trust for now I've have no need
stray

Love is...

Love is blind

Love is kind

It's also what my heart's destine to find

The one true thing that makes us feel secure and free

I know you're the one for me

Real love...

My love is like an overflowing stream its real

Not an illusion or dream

I can't get caught in the wave

Cause I'd have to choose to swim,

Sink, or be saved

Put in check...

No longer will my heart rejected

I'm in love with a player

And I'm about to check him

Now I've learned a thing or two

And that is ... I can have you

On a bus, on a train, in a bathroom stall

How about we try it in the lingerie department at the mall

I don't want this to be just a one night fling

I want it to end with a ring

Not around my head

But on my finger instead

Now you can wait too late

But I'm telling you no longer will I wait

Kinky...

How often must I try

To hold back and deny

The love for you is so real

I want the superb deal

This thing is so great

There will never be a debate

Of the love that I have for you

What's a kinky girl to do

I wanna lick you lips

While you suck on my nips

Then mess up the bed spread

Shit lets go for a new head board for the bed

I want to shiver and quiver

As if I just dived into a cold winter river

Picked...

Sometimes I feel as if life is like a rose

Always smelly or patiently waiting to be chose

But often it makes us happy or sometimes cries

We just to analyze and figure out which one and why

There are no words to explain the unexpected course

Just have to pray they don't go from good to worse

My life is such a deep hollow hole

Much like a wounded heart weary and cold

Thou I try to find the love that is respectful and kind

My long lost search will never end

For this is just the beginning of my search

For any lonely, sexy romantic men

Still waiting...

How do I address the fact?

That my life is not completely in tact

I'm still not with you

Yes it's true

That my gray cloud will never be blue

I will survive

And keep hope alive

That one day

Everything will fast forward to play

The misery will end

Words of wisdom just don't give in to sin

In my feelings *Poetry*

www.ingramcontent.com/pod-product-compliance
Lightning Source LLC
LaVergne TN
LVHW051427080426
835508LV00022B/3276